COUNTRY PROFILES

MADAGASCAR

BY GOLRIZ GOLKAR

BLASTOFF! DISCOVERY

BELLWETHER MEDIA • MINNEAPOLIS, MN

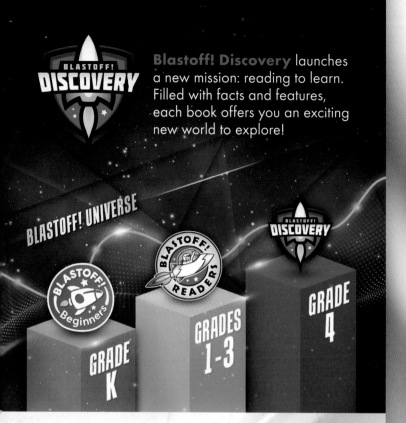

Blastoff! Discovery launches a new mission: reading to learn. Filled with facts and features, each book offers you an exciting new world to explore!

BLASTOFF! UNIVERSE

BLASTOFF! Beginners — GRADE K

BLASTOFF! READERS — GRADES 1-3

BLASTOFF! DISCOVERY — GRADE 4

This edition first published in 2021 by Bellwether Media, Inc.

No part of this publication may be reproduced in whole or in part without written permission of the publisher.
For information regarding permission, write to Bellwether Media, Inc.,
Attention: Permissions Department,
6012 Blue Circle Drive, Minnetonka, MN 55343.

Library of Congress Cataloging-in-Publication Data

Names: Golkar, Golriz, author.
Title: Madagascar / by Golriz Golkar.
Other titles: Blastoff! discovery. Country profiles.
Description: Minneapolis, MN : Bellwether Media, 2021. |
    Series: Blastoff! discovery: Country profiles | Includes
    bibliographical references and index.
Audience: Ages 7-13 | Audience: Grades 4-6 | Summary: "Engaging
    images accompany information about Madagascar. The combination
    of high-interest subject matter and narrative text is intended for
    students in grades 3 through 8" –Provided by publisher.
Identifiers: LCCN 2020049051 (print) | LCCN 2020049052 (ebook)
    | ISBN 9781644874493 (library binding) | ISBN
    9781648341267 (ebook)
Subjects: LCSH: Madagascar–Juvenile literature.
Classification: LCC DT469.M28 G65 2021 (print) | LCC DT469.M28
    (ebook) | DDC 969.1–dc23
LC record available at https://lccn.loc.gov/2020049051
LC ebook record available at https://lccn.loc.gov/2020049052

Editor: Kieran Downs   Designer: Laura Sowers

Printed in the United States of America, North Mankato, MN.

TABLE OF CONTENTS

QUEEN'S PALACE

ANTANANARIVO

A family passes through the beautiful stone gate at the Queen's Palace. Perched high on a hill, this ancient part of the Rovä offers a sweeping view of Antananarivo. After visiting the other palaces of the Rovä, they stop to admire the impressive tombs of Madagascar's rulers.

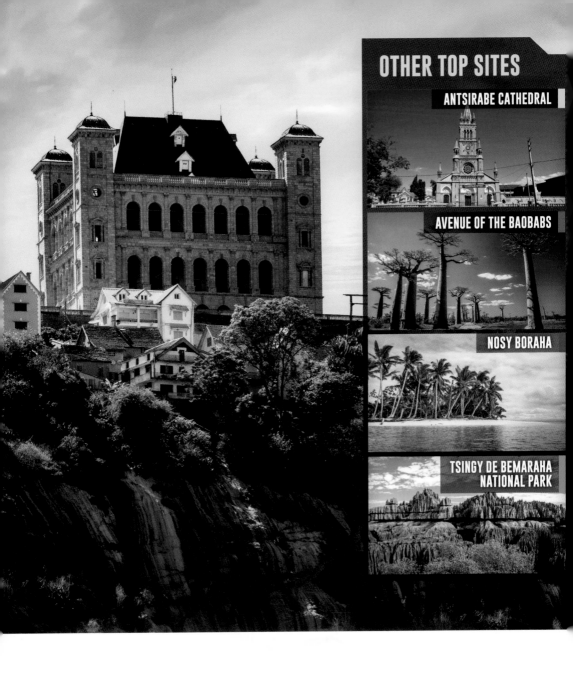

OTHER TOP SITES

ANTSIRABE CATHEDRAL

AVENUE OF THE BAOBABS

NOSY BORAHA

TSINGY DE BEMARAHA NATIONAL PARK

Back in the city, the family visits a *hotely* for lunch. They eat a delicious *poulet* dish made from rice, chicken, and tomato. Afterwards, they head to Lemurs' Park. Ring-tailed and bamboo lemurs climb the trees as tortoises and geckos roam the ground below. From historical sites to amazing wildlife, Madagascar is an island of beauty!

COMOROS

- - - MAYOTTE

NOSY BE

THE BIG ISLAND
Madagascar is the fourth-largest island in the world.

MADAGASCAR

ANTANANARIVO

NOSY BORAHA

MOZAMBIQUE CHANNEL

TOAMASINA

ANTSIRABE

FIANARANTSOA

INDIAN OCEAN

Madagascar is an island country that covers 226,658 square miles (587,041 square kilometers). It is located off the southeastern coast of Africa in the Indian Ocean. The Mozambique Channel separates Madagascar from **mainland** Africa to the west. Madagascar's closest neighboring country is the island nation of Comoros. It lies northwest of Madagascar. The French territories of Mayotte and Réunion Island are also nearby.

The capital, Antananarivo, is located in the center of the island. Madagascar has several small islands as well. They include Nosy Be near the northwestern coast and Nosy Boraha near the northeastern coast.

LANDSCAPE AND CLIMATE

Madagascar features a **diverse** landscape surrounding a large central **plateau**. In the north, sandy beaches stretch across the coast. Hills and rocky slopes dominate the west. The Mangoky River runs across the country and drains into the Mozambique Channel. The rocky Andringitra **Massif** runs through the southeastern deserts. The Atsinanana **rain forest** lies along the eastern coast. The inland Tsaratanana Massif peaks at Mount Maromokotro.

= ANDRINGITRA MASSIF
= ATSINANANA RAIN FOREST

N
W + E
S

MANGOKY RIVER

ANDRINGITRA MASSIF

ATSINANANA
RAIN FOREST

ANTANANARIVO

Average
seasonal highs
and lows

JANUARY
HIGH: 80 °F (27 °C)
LOW: 63 °F (17 °C)

APRIL
HIGH: 78 °F (26 °C)
LOW: 61 °F (16 °C)

JULY
HIGH: 68 °F (20 °C)
LOW: 50 °F (10 °C)

OCTOBER
HIGH: 79 °F (26 °C)
LOW: 57 °F (14 °C)

°F = degrees Fahrenheit
°C = degrees Celsius

Madagascar's coasts have a **tropical** climate.
Inland Madagascar has a **temperate** climate.
Summers are hot and rainy, while winters are cooler
and dry. Mountainous areas have cold winters.

Most of the plants and animals found in Madagascar are not found anywhere else in the world. Fossas hunt for aye-ayes hiding in the rain forest trees. Ring-tailed lemurs, the national animal, search for fruits and leaves to eat. Panther chameleons crawl along the forest floor, looking for crickets and worms. Blue couas chirp from their branches.

Flamingos and herons splash in lakes and ponds. Madagascan fish eagles soar above the water searching for fish such as sea bream and flagtails. Hammerhead sharks and humpback whales swim the coastal waters. They hunt for tuna and small fish.

FOSSA

GREATER FLAMINGO

WEST INDIAN OCEAN COELACANTH

PANTHER CHAMELEON

LIVING FOSSILS

Coelacanths are a species of fish that lived at the same time as dinosaurs. Today, the West Indian Ocean Coelacanth can be found in the ocean waters around Madagascar.

RING-TAILED LEMURS

RING-TAILED LEMUR

Life Span: up to 18 years
Red List Status: endangered

ring-tailed lemur range =

LEAST CONCERN	NEAR THREATENED	VULNERABLE	ENDANGERED	CRITICALLY ENDANGERED	EXTINCT IN THE WILD	EXTINCT

A MIXED LANGUAGE

Malagasy is a mix of Indonesian, Arabic, Malaysian, and African languages.

Nearly 27 million people live in Madagascar. They are called Malagasy. About 9 out of 10 people in Madagascar are part of the Malagasy **ethnic** group. This group is broken down into 20 smaller groups including the Merina, Betsimisaraka, and Betsileo. Other ethnic groups include people with French, Chinese, or Indo-Pakistani **ancestors**.

About 4 out of every 10 Malagasy have **native** religious beliefs. They believe in a **supreme** being and that their ancestors are messengers between the gods and the living. Half of the population practices Christianity. A small group is Muslim. Malagasy and French are the country's two official languages.

FAMOUS FACE

Name: Jean-Luc Raharimanana
Birthday: June 26, 1967
Hometown: Antananarivo, Madagascar
Famous for: Award-winning writer who has written poems and short stories about Madagascar, and who has also worked as a professor and journalist

SPEAK MALAGASY

ENGLISH	MALAGASY	HOW TO SAY IT
hello	manao ahoana	mah-NOW ow-oh-nah
goodbye	veloma	ve-LOOM-uh
please	aza fady	a-za FAAD-ee
thank you	misaotra	mis-OW-tra
yes	eny	EH-nee
no	tsia	TZEE-uh

ANTANANARIVO

COMMUNITIES

Most Malagasy live in **rural** areas. In the highlands, houses are large and made of clay. Coastal homes are smaller and raised above the ground to prevent flood damage. Rural families usually sleep in one room. They travel on foot or by bus. Most **urban** Malagasy live in Antananarivo. Houses usually have two floors. Some Malagasy live in shacks. Vans called bush taxis provide transportation between large towns.

The Malagasy value their families. Relatives often live near each other. Children live at home until marriage. They later move in with their husband's or wife's family.

The Malagasy are very polite and social. They enjoy visiting friends and family. Gifts and food are usually offered. Elderly people are highly respected and greeted first. Older men may deliver speeches called *kabary* at gatherings. These speeches are an important part of Malagasy **culture**. They are also given during weddings, burials, and business events.

Malagasy culture considers many things to be *fady*, or **taboo**. Common taboos forbid people from eating certain foods or visiting specific places. Every village has its own fady to live by. Even families have their own rules.

Children in Madagascar must attend school from ages 6 to 10. Primary school is taught in Malagasy. Secondary school is taught in French. **Poverty** prevents most children from finishing school. Those who finish and pass an exam may attend universities or trade schools.

Most Malagasy work in agriculture. Many are farmers. They raise crops such as coffee, peanuts, and beans. Others may work on vanilla, rice, or banana **plantations**. Some workers find jobs in factories. Educated Malagasy may find jobs in science, research, and business. However, it is often very hard to find work in these areas.

RICE FARMERS

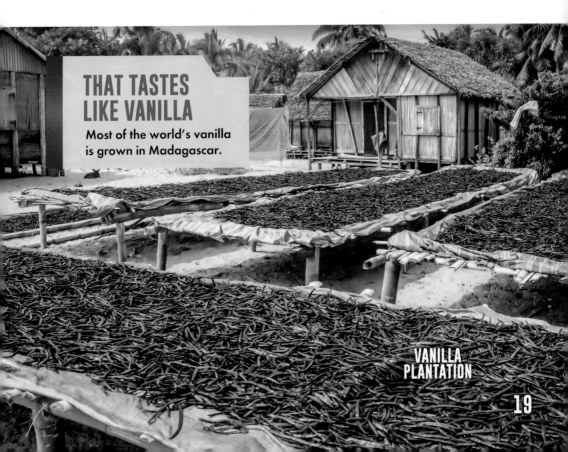

THAT TASTES LIKE VANILLA

Most of the world's vanilla is grown in Madagascar.

VANILLA PLANTATION

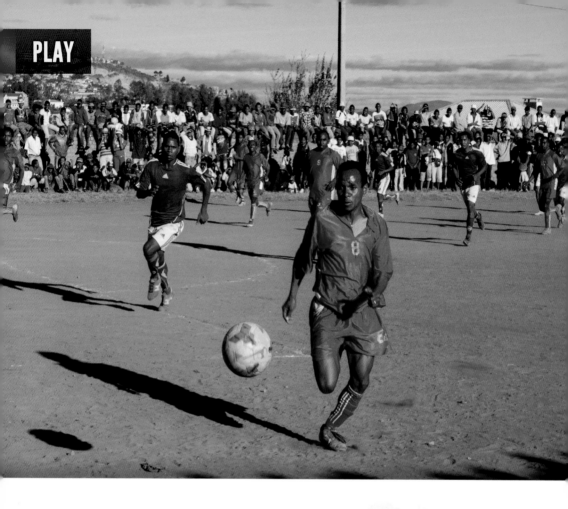

Soccer is the most popular sport in Madagascar. Many local villages have their own teams. Basketball is popular, too. Other national sports include track and field, tennis, judo, and boxing. Malagasy professional athletes have played in the Olympic Games. Many Malagasy enjoy watching a **traditional** form of wrestling called *moraingy*.

MORAINGY

20

Music and movies are popular in Madagascar. Urban residents attend outdoor concerts and dance in nightclubs. Small towns set up temporary video houses where people watch movies. The Malagasy also enjoy dominoes and board games like *fanorona*. Children often make their own toys from found objects.

FANORONA

PÉTANQUE

Also called *boules*, this fun game was invented in France and is enjoyed in Madagascar by people of all ages.

What You Need:
- a small ball that does not bounce called the jack
- 12 larger balls, about the size of a tennis ball
- a yard stick
- 4 players

Instructions:
1. Draw a circle to stand in. Each player will throw from this circle.
2. While standing in the circle, a player from the first team throws the jack.
3. The other player on the first team throws a ball, trying to get as close to the jack as possible.
4. After the first team throws, the second team throws a ball. They can try to get closer to the jack or knock the first team's ball farther away from it.
5. If the second team gets closer to the jack, the first team throws again. Teams switch who is throwing if the team that is closer to the jack changes. Each player gets to throw three balls.
6. Once all 12 balls have been thrown, the team that is closest to the jack wins the round. They get a point for every ball that is closer to the jack than the other team's closest ball. The first team to score 13 points wins!

BANANA SPOONS
Many Malagasy in rural areas use folded banana leaves to scoop up and eat their food.

Rice is a **staple** in almost every Malagasy meal. A traditional breakfast may be either rice soup or deep-fried pancakes called *mofo gasy* served with coffee. For lunch and dinner, rice is eaten with *laoka*. These may include meat, fish, or vegetables with spices.

Ravitoto stew is prepared with pork or zebu, a kind of beef. It is served with coconut and greens. The national dish, *romazava*, features zebu in a spicy tomato sauce with mixed greens. Fish is usually grilled or fried. For dessert, fresh fruit may be served with rice tea called *ranonapango*.

MOFO GASY

ROMAZAVA

MALAGASY CAKE

This light and sweet banana cake makes a perfect dessert or snack! Ask an adult to help you make this recipe.

Ingredients:

2 cups milk

1 vanilla pod

4 tablespoons sugar

1 tablespoon butter

1 pinch ground nutmeg

1 pinch crushed clove

5 tablespoons tapioca

2 tablespoons heavy cream

4 very ripe bananas

4 eggs

Steps:

1. Mix the milk, nutmeg, clove, sugar, and vanilla pod in a saucepan over high heat and bring to a boil.

2. Remove the saucepan from the stove and add the tapioca.

3. Place the saucepan over low heat. Allow to cook for ten minutes while stirring occasionally.

4. Preheat the oven to 350 degrees Fahrenheit (177 degrees Celsius).

5. Remove the saucepan from the heat. Take out the vanilla pod and add the cream.

6. Mash the bananas well with a fork and add to the cake batter.

7. Add the eggs one by one to the cake batter and mix well.

8. Grease a round or loaf cake pan with butter and pour in the cake batter.

9. Bake for 15 minutes. Remove from oven and serve warm.

CELEBRATIONS

There are two different New Year's celebrations in Madagascar. In addition to the January 1 holiday, the Malagasy celebrate *Alahamadi Be* in March. This traditional new year celebrates the year's first rice harvest. For two days, the Malagasy celebrate with special meals, street music, and family visits.

Easter is the most important Christian holiday in Madagascar. People visit church and enjoy a large lunch before visiting friends and family. In June, Independence Day is celebrated with big meals, parades, and games. The night before celebrations begin, Malagasy children walk the streets with lanterns and candles. Madagascar honors its rich culture all year long!

INDEPENDENCE DAY PARADE

HIRA GASY

Hira Gasy are traditional Malagasy musical performances. They began in the Malagasy royal court. Today, Hira Gasy are held during ceremonies or for entertainment events.

1500
Portuguese explorers are the first Europeans to come to Madagascar

AROUND 500
Indo-Malayans migrate to Madagascar from Indonesia and Malaysia

1896
France takes power over Madagascar, sending Malagasy royalty into exile

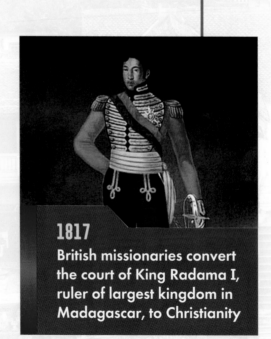

1817
British missionaries convert the court of King Radama I, ruler of largest kingdom in Madagascar, to Christianity

1960
Madagascar becomes independent from France, electing Philibert Tsiranana as its first president

2009
Andry Rajoelina replaces President Ravalomanana after violent protests occur across the country

1992
President Ratsiraka introduces democratic reforms and a new constitution is written

2017
Madagascar experiences an outbreak of the bubonic plague

2005
Madagascar receives money from the United States to continue improving its government and economy

Official Name: Republic of Madagascar

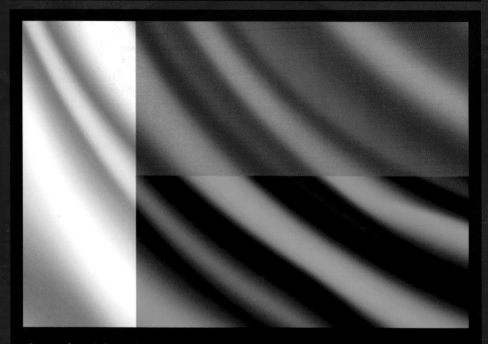

Flag of Madagascar: The Malagasy flag has a vertical white band on the left and two horizontal bands on the right. The top band is red, and the bottom band is green. The white band represents purity, the red band represents Madagascar's independent government, and the green band represents hope.

Area: 226,658 square miles (587,041 square kilometers)

Capital City: Antananarivo

Important Cities: Fianarantsoa, Toamasina, Antsirabe

Population: 26,955,737 (July 2020)

WHERE PEOPLE LIVE

COUNTRYSIDE 38.5%

CITY 61.5%

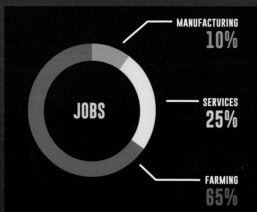

MANUFACTURING
10%

JOBS

SERVICES
25%

FARMING
65%

Main Exports:

vanilla

coffee

sugarcane

clothes

National Holiday:
Independence Day (June 26)

Main Languages:
Malagasy, French

Form of Government:
semi-presidential republic

Title for Country Leaders:
president (head of state)
prime minister (head of government)

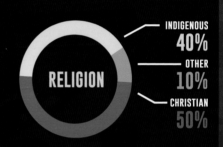

RELIGION

INDIGENOUS
40%

OTHER
10%

CHRISTIAN
50%

Unit of Money:
Malagasy ariary

GLOSSARY

ancestors—relatives who lived long ago

culture—the beliefs, arts, and ways of life in a place or society

diverse—made up of people or things that are different from one another

ethnic—related to a group of people who share customs and an identity

mainland—a continent or main part of a continent

massif—a tightly packed group of mountains

native—originally from the area or related to a group of people that began in the area

plantations—large farms that grow coffee beans, cotton, rubber, or other crops; plantations are mainly found in warm climates.

plateau—an area of flat, raised land

poverty—the lack of money or possessions

rain forest—a thick, green forest that receives a lot of rain

rural—related to the countryside

staple—a widely used food or other item

supreme—highest in rank or authority

taboo—prohibited due to social custom

temperate—associated with a mild climate that does not have extreme heat or cold

traditional—related to customs, ideas, or beliefs handed down from one generation to the next

tropical—part of the tropics; the tropics is a hot, rainy region near the equator.

urban—related to cities and city life

TO LEARN MORE

AT THE LIBRARY

Heale, Jay. *Madagascar.* New York, N.Y.:
Cavendish Square Publishing, 2017.

Klepeis, Alicia Z. *South Africa.* Minneapolis, Minn.:
Bellwether Media, 2021.

Orr, Tamra B. *Madagascar.* New York, N.Y.:
Children's Press, 2017.

ON THE WEB

FACTSURFER

Factsurfer.com gives you
a safe, fun way to find
more information.

1. Go to www.factsurfer.com.

2. Enter "Madagascar" into the search box
   and click Q.

3. Select your book cover to see a list
   of related content.

INDEX

The images in this book are reproduced through the courtesy of: KENTA SUDO, cover; Artush, pp. 4-5; Hemis/ Alamy Stock Photo, p. 5 (Antsirabe Cathedral); Pav-Pro Photography Ltd, p. 5 (Avenue of the Baobabs); pierivb, p. 5 (Nosy Boraha); Pierre-Yves Babelon, pp. 5 (Tsingy de Bemaraha National Park), 14, 17, 24-25; Katya Tsvetkova, p. 8; Sergey Mayorov, p. 9; Dudarev Mikhail, p. 9 (Antananarivo); The Africa Image Library/ Alamy Stock Photo, p. 10 (fossa); Ondrej Prosicky, p. 10 (greater flamingo); mauritius images GmbH/ Alamy, p. 10 (West Indian Ocean coelacanth); CathyKeifer, p. 10 (panther chameleon); Sjo, pp. 10-11; Nok Lek, p. 12; Sandrine Constant/ Wikipedia, p. 13 (top); milosk50, p. 13 (bottom); Artush, p. 15; Lubo Ivanko, p. 16; Dietmar Temps, p. 18; robertharding/ Alamy Stock Photo, p. 19 (top); Panther Media GmbH/ Alamy Stock Photo, p. 19 (bottom); guichaoua/ Alamy Stock Photo, p. 20 (top); Hery Zo Rakotondramanana/ Wikipedia, p. 20 (bottom); JHNRA/ Alamy Stock Photo, p. 21 (top); azur13, p. 21 (bottom); Ron Emmons/ Alamy Stock Photo, p. 22; Lamyai, p. 22 (banana leaves); Boaz Rottem/ Alamy Stock Photo, p. 23 (*mofo gasy*); onella Andriamahery, p. 23 (*romazava*); gaelgogo, p. 23 (malagasy cake); Xinhua/ Alamy Stock Photo, pp. 24, 27 (right); Philippe-Auguste Ramanankirahina/ Wikipedia, p. 26; Service de Presse et d'Information/ Wikipedia, p. 27 (left); Prachaya Roekdeethaweesab, p. 29 (banknote); money & coins @ ian sanders/ Alamy Stock Photo, p. 29 (coin).